A Comprehensive Plan That Reduces Gun Violence and Respects the 2nd Amendment Rights of

Law-Abiding Americans

IT'S TIME TO ACT: A COMPREHENSIVE PLAN THAT REDUCES GUN VIOLENCE AND RESPECTS THE 2ND AMENDMENT RIGHTS OF LAW-ABIDING AMERICANS

Executive Summary

On January 16, 2013, President Obama signed a series of executive actions that will have a meaningful impact on reducing gun violence. However, reducing gun violence cannot be the job of only one branch of government. The policies that will have the greatest impact require congressional action. It's time for Congress to act.

For nearly two months, the Gun Violence Prevention Task Force, under the leadership of Chairman Mike Thompson, has met with people on both sides of the aisle and all sides of the issue to develop a comprehensive set of policy principles that respect the 2nd Amendment and will make our schools, neighborhoods, and communities safer.

The task force met with and solicited input from victims of gun violence and gun safety advocates; gun owners, hunters, and outdoor sportsmen; federal, state, and local law enforcement; educators and community workers; mental health experts and physicians; representatives of the motion picture, television, music, and video game industries; leaders in our faith communities; and representatives of gun manufacturers and retailers, as well as cabinet secretaries and the Vice President of the United States. The task force also met with Members of Congress from all sides of the issue, and held hearings in Washington, DC to consider ways to address this issue.

There is no law or set of laws that will completely end gun violence, but that cannot be an excuse to do nothing. Chairman Thompson and the Gun Violence Prevention Task Force urge Congress to:

➢ **Support the 2nd Amendment rights of law-abiding Americans.** The United States Supreme Court affirmed individuals' 2nd rights to firearms in *District of Columbia v. Heller* (2008). However, the Supreme Court also held that "the right secured by the Second Amendment is not unlimited," Within the limits described by *Heller*, the federal government has the responsibility to take appropriate steps to protect our citizens from gun violence.

➢ **Support citizens' rights to possess firearms for hunting, shooting sports, defense, and other lawful and legitimate purposes:** In the United States, there is a long tradition of hunting and recreational shooting, and firearms are often passed down within families from generation to generation. Policies passed by Congress should respect this.

➢ **Reinstate and strengthen a prospective federal ban on assault weapons:** These weapons are designed to fire a large number of rounds in a short period of time. They constitute a lethal threat to law enforcement and other first responders.

➢ **Reinstate a prospective federal ban on assault magazines:** These magazines hold more than ten rounds and allow a shooter to inflict mass damage in a short period of time without reloading. Banning them will save lives.

➢ **Require a background check for every gun sale, while respecting reasonable exceptions for cases such as gifts between family members and temporary loans for sporting purposes:** It is estimated that four out of ten gun buyers do not go through a background check when purchasing a firearm because federal law only requires these checks when someone buys a gun from a federally licensed dealer. That would be like allowing four out of ten people to choose if they'd go through airport security. This loophole allows felons, domestic abusers, and those prohibited because of mental illness to easily bypass the criminal background check system and buy firearms at gun shows, through private sellers, over the internet or out of the trunks of cars.

➢ **Strengthen the National Instant Criminal Background Check System (NICS) database:** Immediate action is needed to ensure the information in the NICS database is up to date. Many federal and state agencies remain deficient in transferring important records to the database. Without the information, the background checks aren't complete. This needs to change.

➢ **Prosecute those prohibited buyers who attempt to purchase firearms and others who violate federal firearm laws:** Federal law bars nine categories of people—including felons and those prohibited because of mental illness —from buying guns. But when prohibited persons attempt to buy guns, they are hardly ever prosecuted. More can and must be done to make these investigations and prosecutions a priority.

➢ **Pass legislation aimed specifically at cracking down on illegal gun trafficking and straw-purchasing:** Straw-purchasing is when a prohibited buyer has someone with no criminal history walk into a gun store, pass a background check and purchase a gun with the purpose of giving it to the prohibited buyer. This puts guns in the hands of people who are prohibited from having them. Congress should pass a law that will put an end to this practice.

➢ **Restore funding for public safety and law enforcement initiatives aimed at reducing gun violence:** Congress should fund law enforcement's efforts to reduce gun violence, while supporting federal research into causes of gun violence. Put simply, there is no reason the Centers for Disease Control (CDC) or the National Institute of Health (NIH) should be inhibited from researching the causes of gun violence. And there is no reason for the restrictions federal law places on our law enforcement officers' ability to track and combat the spread of illegal guns.

➢ **Support initiatives that prevent problems before they start: Local communities should have assistance in applying evidence-based prevention and early intervention strategies that are** designed to prevent the problems that lead to gun violence before those problems start.

➢ **Close the holes in our mental-health system and make sure that care is available for those who need it:** Congress must improve prevention, early intervention, and treatment of mental illness while working to eliminate the stigma associated with mental illness. Access to mental health services should be improved, the shortage of mental health professionals should be addressed, and funding should be made available for those programs that have proven to be effective.

➢ **Help our communities get unwanted and illegal guns out of the hands of those who don't want them or shouldn't have them:** Congress should help support and develop local programs that get unwanted guns off our streets. And Congress should work with states to develop programs that get guns out of the hands of those convicted of certain crimes or those prohibited because of mental illness.

➢ **Support responsible gun ownership:** Congress should support safety training, research aimed at developing new gun safety technologies and the safe storage of firearms.

➢ **Take steps to enhance school safety.** Congress must help all schools implement evidence-based strategies that support safe learning environments tailored to the unique needs of students and local communities. And Congress must work with all schools to develop emergency response plans.

➢ **Address our culture's glorification of violence seen and heard though our movie screens, television shows, music and video games:** Congress should fund scientific research on the relationship between popular culture and gun violence, while ensuring that parents have access to the information they need to make informed decisions about what their families watch, listen to, and play.

Chairman Thompson is a gun owner, hunter, former co-chair of the Congressional Sportsman Caucus, supporter of the Second Amendment and a combat veteran who carried an assault rifle in Vietnam. He was joined on the Task Force leadership team by 11 vice chairs, representing a range of expertise and backgrounds from all corners of the House Democratic Caucus.

Vice-Chairs of the Task Force are:

● **Rep. Ron Barber (AZ)** – Congressman Ron Barber had a 30-year career with the Division of Developmental Disabilities in the Arizona Department of Economic Security before being elected to the United States Congress. Under his direction, the division improved services for families, while running one of the five most cost-efficient, high-quality programs in the country. After his retirement, Barber became district director for Congresswoman Gabrielle Giffords. He was standing next to her on Jan. 8, 2011 when a gunman opened fire at a Congress on Your Corner event. Barber was shot twice and critically wounded. When Congresswoman Giffords stepped down to focus on her recovery, Barber ran for the seat, winning the right to succeed her in office.

● **Rep. John D. Dingell (MI)** – Congressman John D. Dingell is the Dean of the House of Representatives and a senior member of the House Committee on Energy and Commerce. A lifelong outdoorsman and conservationist, Congressman Dingell is an avid hunter and sportsman and member of the Migratory Bird Conservation Commission. Congressman Dingell is also one of the primary authors of the National Instant Criminal Background Check System Improvement Amendments Act of 2007.

- **Rep. Elizabeth Esty (CT)** – Congresswoman Elizabeth Esty represents Newtown, Connecticut in Congress. In the wake of the Sandy Hook Elementary School tragedy, she has met with first responders, mental health professionals, educators, community leaders, and local elected officials in Newtown. She approaches the need for sensible gun policies as a community leader, attorney, and mother who has served as a room parent for a first-grade classroom. As a member of the Connecticut State House of Representatives, Esty advocated for commonsense legislation to reduce gun violence and keep families safe.

- **Rep. Chaka Fattah (PA)** – Congressman Chaka Fattah serves as the Ranking Member on House Appropriations subcommittee on Commerce, Justice, and Science. Fattah, a major supporter of the ATF, is deeply involved in issues dealing with firearms, public safety and law enforcement. In Philadelphia, PA, where he represents, Fattah created the successful gun buyback "Groceries for Guns" program that has removed thousands of dangerous, unwanted firearms from streets and homes of Philadelphians in exchange for grocery coupons.

- **Rep. Carolyn McCarthy (NY)** – Congresswoman Carolyn McCarthy, a lifelong nurse, focused her efforts to reduce gun violence after her husband was murdered and son critically wounded in the 1993 mass shooting on the Long Island Railroad in New York. Her activism led her to Washington, first to lobby members of Congress as an advocate for victims, and then as a member herself after running against her own Congressman who voted against the 1994 assault weapons ban. Today, McCarthy is the lead author of legislation to ban semiautomatic assault weapons and high-capacity ammunition magazines, close the gun-show loophole, strengthen our national background check database, and ban the anonymous bulk online sale of ammunition.

- **Rep. Grace Napolitano (CA)** – Congresswoman Grace F. Napolitano is the founder and co-chair of the Congressional Mental Health Caucus. In 2001, she secured funding to provide on-site mental health services for schools within her Congressional District, a program that has now expanded to 15 other area schools. Napolitano authored the Mental Health in Schools Act, which would implement on-site mental health services for schools on a national level, and each year has introduced legislation to recognize May as *National Mental Health Awareness Month*. In 2010, Napolitano created the bipartisan Congressional Mental Health Task Force, which includes notable figures such as: Los Angeles Laker, Metta World Peace; World Championship Boxer, Mia St. John, and Dancing with the Stars celebrity, Mark Ballas to help raise awareness about mental health, rid the stigma associated with mental illness, and encourage others to seek help.

- **Rep. Ed Perlmutter (CO)** -- Congressman Ed Perlmutter represents the 7th Congressional District of Colorado encompassing the northern and western suburbs of the Denver metro region. Residents of this district are diverse, moderate and middle of the road with their personal values, economics, and education. Perlmutter represented the City of Aurora, CO during the tragic movie theater shootings in July 2012. He also represented the area surrounding Columbine High School while serving in the Colorado State Senate. Perlmutter has extensive experience in Colorado working to create mandatory criminal background checks for all gun purchases, and during his time in the state Senate, he sponsored many crime control and victims' assistance measures.

- **Rep. David Price (NC)** – Congressman David Price is the Ranking Member of the House Appropriations subcommittee on Homeland Security, where he has worked to improve public safety and ensure first responders have access to the tools they need to protect our communities. As a member of the Congressional Mental Health Caucus, he has long supported robust funding for mental health services and was an early advocate for the Paul Wellstone Mental Health Parity Act, which became law in the 110th Congress. Rep. Price has also supported efforts to keep guns out of the hands of dangerous criminals and limit the sale of military-style weapons.

- **Rep. Bobby Scott (VA)** – Congressman Bobby Scott serves as the Ranking Member of the House Judiciary Subcommittee on Crime, Terrorism, and Homeland Security. He is a known leader of legislative efforts to reduce crime and prevent youth violence by advocating for comprehensive, evidence-based solutions. Towards this goal, he has introduced the Youth PROMISE Act. Following the Columbine tragedy, he co-led a bi-partisan effort to develop juvenile crime prevention and accountability legislation that resulted in the Juvenile Accountability Block Grant Program (JABG) legislation which passed into law in 2002. He has also co-led bipartisan efforts to enable the ATF to more effectively enforce gun sale and transfer regulations and to close the gun show loophole.

- **Rep. Jackie Speier (CA)** – Congresswoman Jackie Speier was Legislative Counsel to Congressman Leo Ryan in 1978 when she accompanied him to investigate the People's Temple cult in Jonestown, Guyana. Congressman Ryan was assassinated, and Speier was shot five times at close range. She still carries two of the bullets in her body. Since that time, she has been a fierce advocate of preventing gun violence including authoring legislation to ban assault weapons while serving as a member of the California State Senate. She supports the 2nd Amendment, but also believes we cannot just blame this crisis on violent video games or mental illness. The proliferation of military style assault weapons and assault magazines are part of the problem, and should be banned. In addition, she believes it is essential that loopholes in the background check process be closed.

- **Rep. Bennie Thompson (MS)** –Congressman Bennie Thompson is an avid hunter and co-chair of the bipartisan Congressional Sportsman's Caucus during the 113th Congress. Congressman Thompson has served as the lead Democrat on the House Committee on Homeland Security since 2007. Prior to his election to Congress, Congressman Thompson served as alderman and mayor of Bolton, Mississippi and as a supervisor in Hinds, County Mississippi.

Introduction

On December 14, 2012, Adam Lanza reportedly killed his mother in her home in Newtown, Connecticut. Lanza then stocked his mother's car with firearms and drove to Sandy Hook Elementary School. Wearing a bulletproof vest and armed with hundreds of rounds of ammunition, he forced his way into the school and opened fire with a .223 Bushmaster semiautomatic assault rifle—equipped with 30-round large-capacity assault magazines—killing 26, including 20 students aged seven and younger. As police closed in, Lanza committed suicide by shooting himself with a handgun.

In the seven weeks since the mass shooting at Sandy Hook Elementary, more than 1480 Americans have been killed by gunfire.

In the wake of this senseless mass shooting, the leadership of the House Democratic Caucus convened this Gun Violence Prevention Task Force, led by Chairman Mike Thompson (CA-05) and eleven Vice Chairs who represent a cross section of positions on the issue of gun violence prevention. Our charge has been to explore the best available methods to address gun violence, to give stakeholders on all sides of this issue a voice in the debate, and to develop common sense principles to guide the U.S. House of Representatives as it works to answer important questions about reducing and preventing gun violence while respecting the Second Amendment rights of law-abiding Americans.

To develop these comprehensive principles, the Task Force solicited the input and testimony of victims of gun violence and gun safety advocates; gun owners, hunters, and outdoor sportsmen; federal, state, and local law enforcement; educators and community workers; mental health experts and physicians; representatives of the motion picture, television, music, and video game industries; leaders in our faith communities; and representatives of gun manufacturers and retailers. We have asked for and received specific policy proposals from Members of Congress. We have met regularly and often to reach the consensus reflected in this document.

The need for action cannot be overstated. Gun violence is a public health crisis of epidemic proportions. In one year, an average of over 100,000 Americans are shot. 32,000 of these individuals die. Nearly 12,000 of these are murdered, which is more than 32 Americans every day, and another 19,000 of these commit suicide using a gun.

Our constituents, our families, and our children deserve to be free from the threat of gun violence in their homes, their schools, and their neighborhoods. We can secure that freedom without encroaching on our constitutional rights. We must work to do so immediately.

And we believe we can do so, by implementing these fifteen, common sense, principles:

I.   The Second Amendment to the United States Constitution guarantees an individual's right to own and possess a firearm for lawful purposes unconnected to service in a militia, including self-defense within the home. The United States Supreme Court articulated this understanding of the law in *District of Columbia v. Heller* (2008). However, the Supreme Court also held that "the right secured by the Second Amendment is not unlimited," and specifically recognized the constitutionality of "prohibiting the carrying of dangerous and unusual weapons." Within the limits described by *Heller*, the federal government has the responsibility to take appropriate steps to protect our citizens from gun violence, and we respect the right of state and local governments to take additional steps to secure their communities. **Consistent with the *Heller* decision, we support the Second Amendment rights of law-abiding individuals.**

II. Most firearms are legally purchased for legitimate purpose. In the United States, there is a long tradition of hunting and recreational shooting, and firearms are often passed down within families from generation to generation. In addition to our support for the rights protected by the Second Amendment, **we recognize that citizens may possess firearms for hunting, shooting sports, defense, and other lawful and legitimate purposes.**

III. Military style semiautomatic assault weapons have been used in a number of mass shootings in our country's history, including the recent tragedies in Aurora, Colorado, and Newtown, Connecticut. These weapons are designed to fire a large number of rounds in a short period of time. They constitute a lethal threat to law enforcement and other first responders. **We support reinstating and strengthening a prospective, federal ban on the sale of additional assault weapons into the civilian market.**

- This ban should target military style semiautomatic assault weapons whose risk to public safety outweighs any sporting or recreational purpose.

- A permanent ban on these assault weapons would be prospective only, and would not apply to firearms already in the possession of lawful gun owners.

- Nevertheless, future transfers of legally-owned assault weapons should be subject to a background check through the NICS system.

IV.   Large capacity ammunition feeding devices, also known as high-capacity assault magazines, that allow a gun to fire more than 10 rounds without reloading, are designed for combat and military purposes, allowing them to be used to kill a large number of people in a short period of time. Limiting the capacity of magazines would allow law enforcement officials the opportunity to stop a crisis situation sooner and save lives. **We support reinstating a prospective federal ban on high-capacity magazines for non-military, non-law enforcement purposes.**

- High-capacity magazines have been used at nearly every mass shooting in the United States for the past thirty years, including at Virginia Tech (2007), Northern Illinois University (2008), Fort Hood (2009), Tucson (2011), Aurora (2012), Oak Creek (2012), and Sandy Hook (2012).

- A ban on large capacity ammunition feeding devices should prohibit the transfer, possession, and importation of such devices manufactured post-enactment, with exceptions for law enforcement and those authorized to test or experiment with such devices.

- Whether or not loaded into high-capacity magazines, armor-piercing bullets pose a particular risk to law enforcement officers and are not needed for civilian use. We support strengthening the laws against "cop killer" bullets.

V.   Today, not all gun purchasers are required to undergo a background check before they are legally able to purchase a gun. Individuals purchasing a firearm have the option of going to a federal firearms licensee (FFL) where a background check will be required, or purchasing a firearm from a private seller without undergoing a check. This alternative has allowed an estimated 6.6 million guns, or about 40 percent of all gun purchases, to be sold each year without the benefit of a federal background check. One critical way to prevent prohibited persons, such as felons, domestic abusers, and those adjudicated ineligible due to mental status, from purchasing firearms is to ensure that the background check system has complete information on individuals that are prohibited from having guns. **We support requiring background checks for all firearms purchases and transfers, with limited exceptions.**

- It is essential that background checks be done quickly and effectively, recognizing both the urgent need for enhanced public safety and the rights of law-abiding gun purchasers.

- As is the case under current law, it is also important that any updated federal background check system not create a national gun registry.

- Finally, although no exception would permit the knowing transfer to anyone prohibited from possessing a firearm, we recognize the benefits of establishing some reasonable exceptions to a universal background check requirement, such as gifts or transfers between family members, inheritances, and temporary loans for sporting purposes.

VI. For the gun purchase background check process to be effective, it is essential that the National Instant Criminal Background Check System (NICS) has relevant and accurate information from all federal and state agencies regarding those prohibited from possessing firearms. Only with this information can NICS be an effective way to determine if a firearms purchaser is eligible to buy and own a gun. However, NICS is missing millions of relevant records due to lax and incomplete reporting by many federal and state agencies. **We support strengthening the NICS database and taking actions to make sure the information in it is up-to-date.**

- The NICS database should be strengthened in a number of ways, including:

  - Enacting new reporting requirements with respect to records indicating disqualification, such as felony convictions and mental health status adjudications, and shortening deadlines for state compliance;

  - Developing an effective and reasonable system to measure the progress of states in uploading records to NICS;

  - Improving reward and penalty provisions to better incentivize the states to share information with NICS;

  - Limiting the authority of the Attorney General to waive state penalties;

  - Clarifying existing mental health definitions; and,

  - Working with states to remove legal barriers that may prevent reporting mental health and other records to NICS.

- In addition, strengthening the NICS database should include working with states to make them aware of best practices for uploading records to NICS. This effort could include a campaign to make states aware of National Criminal History Improvement Program, which can provide states with funds to improve technology and better facilitate the upload of critical records.

VII.   In order for current and future gun laws, including the use of comprehensive background checks, to be maximally successful, we must prosecute those who break the law. Strict enforcement of the law better protects the public from dangerous criminals, many of whom have provided false or incomplete information to licensed firearm dealers. **We support increased prosecutions of persons who violate federal firearms law.**

- Congress must provide the Department of Justice with additional resources to support increased prosecutions of individuals who lie on background check forms and those who engage in other firearms-related crime, and we encourage enhanced cooperative efforts between federal, state, and local law enforcement to pursue firearms criminals.

- We support making more resources available to the Bureau of Alcohol, Tobacco, Firearms, and Explosives (BATFE) to help them properly investigate and responsibly develop cases, and urge the Senate to confirm a permanent Director of BATFE.

- We support additional research to assess and improve the technological means for law enforcement to investigate firearms crimes.

- Finally, we support proactive, community policing strategies to reduce gun violence in all of our communities.

VIII.   Every year, hundreds of thousands of guns enter the illegal market and wind up on our streets and in our communities. Many enter the market through straw purchasers who buy guns from licensed dealers on behalf of criminals, theft of weapons which may go unreported, and corrupt gun dealers, among other reasons. These activities put guns in the hands of persons who are prohibited from having them and those who intend to use them unlawfully. A high percentage of guns used by Mexican drug trafficking organizations come from the United States, and are often purchased, particularly in the Southwest Border states, by straw purchasers buying them on behalf of those planning to transport them to Mexico and elsewhere. Federal law does not adequately prohibit or punish these activities. **We support enacting a new federal law that explicitly prohibits gun trafficking and straw purchasing.**

- Under current federal law, straw purchasing is prosecuted through a statute that prohibits lying on federal firearms paperwork, an offense which does not adequately reflect the seriousness of the injection of firearms into the illegal market by straw purchasers.

- A new firearms trafficking statute should create stiff penalties for these serious crimes, but should not affect any legitimate gun owner's ability to buy or use a firearm.

IX.   Over the last 20 years, Congress has imposed strict limitations on certain federal programs, law enforcement activities, and research related to gun violence and community safety. Congress has also sharply decreased funding for these activities. These limitations have hindered federal agencies and their state, local, and non-governmental partners from studying gun violence, minimizing gun violence, and enforcing the law. **We support restoring adequate federal funding to public safety programs and removing barriers that inhibit the use of federal funds on gun violence prevention and research.**

- Congress must protect and increase funding for programs that are designed to help make our neighborhoods and schools safer. These programs include (1) the Edward Bryne Justice Assistant Grant (JAG) Program; (2) Community Oriented Policing Service (COPS) Program; (3) NICS Improvement Program; (4) the Office of Juvenile Justice and Delinquency Prevention (OJJDP); and (5) the Secure Our Schools Program.

- It is imperative for federal agencies to collect data and conduct research on gun violence. Sound scientific information will inform better policy decisions and improve both public health and public safety. Current funding restrictions, which on their face prevent only advocacy for gun control, has had the consequence of chilling all federal research on gun violence. Specifically, we must:

    1. Remove the Dickey Restrictions. Since 1996, Congress has prohibited the Centers for Disease Control (CDC) from using taxpayer funds to "advocate or promote gun control," leading CDC to effectively halt all research into the causes and prevention of gun violence. Research of this nature does not inherently constitute advocacy for or the promotion of gun control, and we support funding federal efforts to conduct science-based, peer-reviewed research into the causes of gun violence in our communities.

    2. Remove the Rehberg Restrictions. In 2011, Congress extended the Dickey prohibition to research conducted by the National Institutes of Health (NIH). Gun violence is a public health and safety issue, and research into methods to improve public safety could help to identify the causes of gun violence and strategies to prevent gun violence.

- Under the Patient Protection and Affordable Care Act, a wellness or health promotion activity cannot require the disclosure or collection of any information relating to the lawful use, possession or storage of a firearm or ammunition by an individual. Some have interpreted this to mean that doctors and other healthcare providers cannot talk with their patients about guns and gun safety, or warn law enforcement authorities about specific threats of violence. Congress should clarify this provision to make clear that it does not prohibit communication between doctors and patients about gun safety, or the reporting of direct and credible threats of violence to the proper authorities.

- The Tiahrt Amendments place a number of different restrictions on federal, state, and local law enforcement authorities that hinder their ability to track and combat the spread of illegal guns. These restrictions primarily: (1) require the destruction of NICS background check records within 24 hours; (2) prevent ATF from requiring that federally licensed dealers perform physical inventory checks to detect lost or stolen guns; (3) restrict access to firearm trace or multiple gun sales report data to local and state enforcement authorities; and (4) prohibits the release of gun trace data except in the course of a criminal investigation. In the aggregate, these restrictions hinder law enforcement's ability to track sellers of illegal guns, track gun trafficking patterns, and catch firearms dealers who falsify their records. We should remove the Tiahrt Amendments because they unnecessarily restrict the ability of law enforcement to maintain public safety.

X. Each day, an average of 47 children and youth are shot, and 8 of them die from their wounds. Another 5 children die each day from abuse or neglect. Comprehensive, evidence-based prevention and early intervention strategies directed toward at-risk youth and families have been scientifically proven to prevent such violence and abuse in a highly cost-effective manner. **We support initiatives that will enable local communities to apply evidence-based prevention and early intervention strategies that contribute to the health, productivity and safety of children, families and the community.**

- Comprehensive, evidence-based prevention and intervention programs directed toward at-risk youth and families both reduce crime and save money. We support these programs. They should be administered according to a plan developed by representatives from local law enforcement, schools, court services, social services, health and mental health services, businesses, and other community organizations.

- We fear that the more commonly taken approach of addressing crime with "tough on crime" strategies after the crimes occur is not only ineffective, but also very costly.

- The U.S. leads the world in incarceration rate and spends over $80 billion a year in incarceration and other correctional costs. By intervening in communities before crimes occur, we can recoup these costs in addition to saving lives.

XI. The vast majority of people living with mental illness are not violent and are far more likely to be victims of crime then perpetrators of crime. If undiagnosed and/or left untreated, mental illness can have serious implications for the individual, their families, and our communities. Early prevention and detection are key to ensuring early and appropriate care, and increases in mental health resources, treatment, and care are critical components to building a stronger mental health system for all Americans. **We support increasing awareness, prevention, early identification, and treatment of mental illness, improving access to mental health services, and efforts to eliminate the stigma associated with mental health diagnosis and treatment.**

- We must ensure mental health parity. Specifically, we urge the Administration to fully enact mental health parity without delay. Doing so will ensure that insurance companies do not discriminate against those with a mental illness.

- More must be done to address the issue of stigma related to mental illness. We must begin a national dialogue on the issue of mental health and wellness to properly educate individuals on what mental health is, how to recognize warning signs and risk factors, and how to access mental health services and resources.

- We must fund and prioritize evidence-based programs and practices for School Based Mental Health Programs. Doing so provides for on-site behavioral health services in schools K-12, while funding prevention and early intervention services to help identify the onset of mental illness at an early age, and providing access to on-site mental health professionals that can adequately address the needs of students. This effort must also include expanded mental health services and resources for post-secondary schools.

- We must also adequately fund mental health programs related to military service members, veterans, and minority communities. All Americans should have access to these essential services and resources.

- Additional efforts must be made to expand the mental health care network generally, including to institutional based and community based mental health treatment specifically. This should include greater investment in Federally Qualified Behavioral Health Centers, among others.

- We must also fund and deploy effective jail diversion programs to better address and identify the appropriate mental health and rehabilitation services for federal and state inmates who have a diagnosable mental health problem. This is essential to address mental health and wellness needs, deter recidivism rates, and to prevent the improper incarceration for those living with a mental illness.

- Congress must also ensure that successful programs, like mental health first aid training, are made available for students, parents, educators, faculty and staff, law enforcement, emergency response personnel, community faith leaders, and others who interact with at-risk populations. These training programs will allow for a greater understanding of mental health warning signs, risk factors, addressing the mental health stigma, and how to access critical mental health resources.

- It is also necessary that our families, schools, and communities have the resources and training they need to put in place evidence-based emergency protocols to address school violence and mental health crisis situations as soon as they develop.

- We are very concerned about the shortage of mental health professionals. We fear that this shortage has contributed to the current mental health crisis by limiting access to resources and services, especially in rural areas. Congress must provide the funding necessary to help increase the mental health workforce, especially for those mental health professionals who work with children, youth, military, veterans, and minority communities; provide adequate pay for mental health professionals; and increase the number of mental health professionals who are educated, trained, and licensed to work with those currently being underserved.

- We also firmly believe that regular assessments should be made on mental health information sharing and program funding to ensure these programs' effectiveness over time.

- Finally, more must be done to work with the media on how to address the subject of mental health and to ensure that the public is properly informed on this important issue. The media is a powerful tool and if done correctly, can reach a high number of Americans to get them the information needed about mental health resources and to eliminate the stigma associated with mental illness.

XII.   Many of our citizens possess unneeded, unwanted, or illegally owned firearms. These firearms include weapons that are no longer being used and are now unwanted by their owner and guns currently owned by once legal gun owners who have become prohibited from owning a firearm at some point after their background check. It is also essential that those who wish to remain gun owners have the legal and mental capacity to do so, and should that status change, that processes be in place to prevent guns from staying in the hands of those whose conduct or mental health make them ineligible to retain them. **We support reasonable efforts to get unneeded, unwanted, and illegal guns off our streets and out of our communities.**

- For years, local governments have been trying various strategies to better engage local communities in removing illegal or unused guns from their neighborhoods, such as illegal gun tip hotlines and voluntary gun buyback programs administered by municipalities or local law enforcement. Tip lines enable citizens to alert police (either anonymously or for reward) about illegal guns in their communities. Buyback programs, including those executed in cooperation with corporate or other partners, offer financial incentives to individuals who turn in their unwanted or unneeded guns.

- Congress should take measures to encourage state and local governments to use federal funds, such as those administered by the Departments of Justice (e.g. Byrne Justice Assistance Grant Program), and others, for innovative and voluntary gun violence reduction programs such as illegal gun tip hotlines and gun buyback programs.

- Over time, gun owners may lose their eligibility to possess a weapon under state or federal law, often because of criminal activity or mental health issues. Innovative programs designed to facilitate the disposal of firearms held by prohibited persons can prevent gun violence. The federal government should encourage states to create and utilize programs that allow local law enforcement to assist gun owners who do not have the legal capacity to own them, in the sale or transfer of their illegal firearms.

XIII.   The majority of firearms are owned and safely operated by responsible gun owners who take seriously their responsibility to our communities. Many gun owners already take it upon themselves to be trained and exercise gun safety best practices.   However, more can and must be done to help gun owners make informed decisions about the safe storage and use of their guns in order to prevent gun violence. Improved efforts should be made to ensure current gun safety technologies are being deployed, while research must also be done to develop new gun safety technologies. **We support the enhancement and promotion of gun safety and owner responsibility.**

- It is essential to start a new national dialogue on responsible gun ownership, which should include a national public service announcement campaign. We should conduct this campaign in coordination with gun owner organizations and other stakeholders. The dialogue should include discussion of the safe storage of firearms, the use of trigger locks and gun safes, steps gun owners should take if their firearm is lost or stolen, and resources pertaining to mental illness and gun ownership, among others.

- We also believe that the federal government should take additional steps to assist in the development and deployment of technology that could minimize gun violence. Specifically, the federal government should encourage in the development and testing of new gun safety technologies and offer greater incentives to encourage the use of currently available safety technologies, like trigger locks, gun safes, and other safe storage options.

- These efforts should not come at the expense of other important conservation programs that are used and closely linked to hunting and shooting sports. This includes programs supported by the Pittman-Robertson Wildlife Restoration Act, the Federal Duck Stamp Program, and the Dingell-Johnson Act, among others. These are long-standing programs that play an essential role in wildlife and habitat protection that must be continued uninterrupted.

XIV. Our schools must be safe environments where teachers, faculty and students can focus on teaching and learning without concerns of any type of violence that detracts from the positive growth of students. While gun violence in schools is rare, any violence in schools is too much and must be addressed. All schools should implement an evidence-based approach to supporting a safe learning environment that is tailored to the unique needs of the students and local communities. To ensure the physical security of our schools, schools should develop safety and emergency response plans to address the physical and emotional safety of all students. Teachers, faculty and other personnel should have the training and supports to implement those plans, including for responding to crisis situations. School policies should go beyond just securing our buildings and campuses and promote a positive school climate that meets both the learning and emotional needs of all students. **We support comprehensive measures to address the physical and emotional safety of students, faculty and staff.**

- While actions to promote safety and prevention at the school level are essential, these policies must be implemented in tandem with comprehensive gun violence prevention initiatives.

- Elementary, secondary and post-secondary schools should collaborate with local community groups to develop and implement a comprehensive, evidence-based safety plan. These groups should include parents, teachers, faculty, student organizations, community based health centers, first-responders and law enforcement. To help facilitate the development and continued implementation of these safety plans, a mechanism should also be established to provide training and research to assist schools at all levels, and to disseminate to them educational public safety information and best practices.

- Meeting the emotional needs of all students is essential to maintain a safe environment. Schools should prioritize policies and supports to promote a positive school climate, including anti-bullying programs and mental health supports.

XV.   Many Americans are concerned that television programs, movies, video games and other forms of media are starting to desensitize young Americans to violence, specifically gun violence, at a very early age. While we have a shared responsibility in this area, it is essential that parents, educators, and our communities at large are aware of and use the tools available to them and that those tools are sufficient to help make informed decisions about the content exposed to our children. While recent scientific research has not demonstrated a causal relationship between modes of entertainment and violence, more research should be done, including with the backing of uninterested government scientists and experts. **We support making available more information about content choices to our parents and communities, and urge that further scientific research be conducted on possible relationships between the depiction of violence in entertainment media and gun violence in our communities.**

- The CDC and other impartial research entities should supplement existing research on the relationship between video games, the media, and gun violence.

- The entertainment and video game industries have a responsibility to give parents the tools to make appropriate choices about what their children watch and play. It is clear to us that these industries take this responsibility seriously. However, as new technologies emerge and new entertainment platforms are developed, Congress must continue to work with these industries to ensure that their efforts remain successful.

House Gun Violence Prevention Task Force Background:

On December 19, 2012, Democratic Leader Nancy Pelosi announced the formation of the House Gun Violence Prevention Task Force and appointed Representative Mike Thompson (CA-05) as chair. The Task Force was charged with developing a comprehensive approach to reduce gun violence and strengthen our nation's gun laws, and to present this plan by early February, 2013.

In the weeks that followed, Chairman Thompson, in consultation with the Task Force leadership team consisting of eleven Vice Chairs representing a range of expertise and backgrounds from all corners of the House Democratic Caucus, worked with their House colleagues and all stakeholders to identify possible solutions to be included in the Task Force's final recommendations. As the Task Force developed these recommendations, their standard was simple: everyone must be at the table, and everything must be on the table for consideration.

It was agreed that for a policy principle to be included in the Task Force's final recommendations, that principle must be supported by at least two-thirds of the 12 member Task Force leadership team. After a series of meetings, public hearings, and lengthy deliberations, each of the 15 policy principles included in this plan met that two-thirds threshold.

On Thursday, February 7, 2013, Chairman Thompson, and the Gun Violence Prevention Task Force leadership team, formally announced their comprehensive plan to reduce gun violence.

House Gun Violence Prevention Task Force Leadership Team:

Chair: Mike Thompson (CA-05)

Vice-Chairs: Ron Barber (AZ-2); John Dingell (MI-12); Elizabeth Esty (CT-5); Chaka Fattah (PA-2); Carolyn McCarthy (NY-4); Grace Napolitano (CA-32); Ed Perlmutter (CO-7); David Price (NC-4); Bobby Scott (VA-3); Jackie Speier (CA-14); Bennie Thompson (MS-2)

Page Intentionally Left Blank

Page Intentionally Left Blank

Page Intentionally Left Blank

Page Intentionally Left Blank